What Families Were Like in

Victorian Times

Fiona Reynoldson

based on an original text by
Richard Wood

HODDER
Wayland

an imprint of Hodder Children's Books

Titles in the
What Families Were Like
series:
Ancient Egypt
Ancient Greece
Roman Britain
Second World War
Tudors and Stuarts
Victorian Times

Designer: Joyce Chester
Consultant: Norah Granger
Editor: Carron Brown
Production controller: Carol Stevens
Picture researcher: Liz Moore

First published in Great Britain in 1998 by
Wayland Publishers Ltd
This paperback edition published in 2002 by
Hodder Wayland, an imprint of Hodder Children's Books
338 Euston Road, London NW1 3BH

Reprinted in 2004

© Hodder Wayland 1998

British Library Cataloguing in Publication Data
Reynoldson, Fiona
Victorian Times.- (What Families were like)
1. Family - Great Britain - History - 19th century -
Juvenile literature 2. Great Britain - Social conditions -
19th century - Juvenile literature
I. Title
306.8 '5 0941 '09034

ISBN 0 7502 4349 X

Typeset in England by Joyce Chester
Printed and bound in China
Text based on *Family Life in Victorian Britain* by Richard Wood
published in 1994 by Wayland Publishers Ltd.

Picture acknowledgements
The Bridgeman Art Library/Christie's *cover* (main),/Private
Collection 20, /Tate Gallery 21; Dr Barnado's 9 (top); Mary Evans
4, 12, 17 (bottom), 19 (bottom); Getty Images 7, 9 (bottom), 10, 11
(bottom), 13 (top), 16, 17 (top), 23 (bottom), 27 (bottom); Billie
Love Historical Collection 11 (top), 15, 18, 19 (top); Archie Miles
cover (right); Norfolk Museums Service *cover* (left), 6, 14 (bottom),
18 (bottom), 22 (bottom), 23 (top), 28, 29; *Punch* 14 (top); Royal
Commission on Historical Monuments in England 13 (bottom);
Salvation Army 8; Trinity College, Cambridge 26; Richard Wood 5.
The remaining pictures are from the Wayland Picture Library.

With thanks to Norfolk Museums Service for providing pictures
from some of their museums.

Contents

Victorian families

Queen Victoria became queen when she was eighteen years old. The year was 1837. In 1840, she married Prince Albert. They enjoyed family life and had nine children. Many ordinary people read about the Queen and her family. They wanted their families to be like hers.

Queen Victoria had nine children. ▼

A time of change

Victoria was queen for more than sixty years. Many things changed during this time. The number of people living in Britain grew enormously.

What was family life really like?

This middle-class family was quite rich. ▼

Queen Victoria's family was rich. The middle-class family in the photograph was quite rich. But many families were very poor. Women, men and children worked long hours. They lived in small, dirty rooms. They were often hungry and cold. Family life was not much fun for poor people.

Home sweet home

Middle-class families lived in big houses. They had servants to cook and clean.

Families with no homes lived on the streets or in a workhouse.

◄ The best room in a middle-class house.

Rich people's homes

The servants and children had bedrooms at the top of the house. A nanny looked after the children. The parents had a bedroom on the first floor.

Sometimes there was also a sitting room on the first floor that was used when visitors came to call. The ladies all dressed up to visit each other. They came to have tea and to talk.

The dining room and study were on the ground floor. The kitchen was at the back of the house. Often it was small and dark. The servants worked there.

Poor people's homes

In Victorian times, more and more people lived in towns. Many people were very poor.

Often poor families lived in one or two filthy rooms. They did not have enough to eat. They often died young.

◄ A poor part of Glasgow in the 1860s.

Working at home

▲ A family working at home making brushes.

In poor families everyone worked. Women worked in the home. They sewed clothes or made things such as gloves or brushes. They worked for fifteen hours a day. Children helped. Fathers went out to work. The family needed every penny to buy food.

In middle-class families, men earned enough money to pay for the family's food, home and servants. Women organised the home.

Children could get free food at a Dr Barnado's home. ▶

People who moved from place to place lived in caravans. ▼

Sleeping on the streets

Dr Barnado came to London in 1866. He was horrified to see hundreds of homeless children. They slept on the streets. He opened special homes where the children could live and be looked after.

The workhouse

Homeless families were sent to a workhouse. Many people had to live there together. Families were split up. They met only once a week for one hour. Life was very hard.

Parents and children

Getting married

Most Victorian people expected to marry and have children. Hardly anybody divorced.

▼ A wedding in 1865.

The wedding

Most poor people married when they were young. Middle-class people waited until they had enough money to have a good home and servants. Middle-class people wore clothes made specially for their wedding. Poor people wore their best clothes to get married.

Road, street etc., and no. or name of house	Name and surname of each person	Relation to head of family	Condition as to marriage	Age	Rank, profession or occupation	Where born
Kent Road 7 Walworth Terrace	James Biggar	Head	Mar	59	Managing Foreman Joiner Retired	Lanarkshire Glasgow
	Mary Biggar	Wife	Mar	56		Stirlingshire Carronshore
	Mary Biggar	Daur	Unm	32	House Keeper	Lanarkshire Glasgow
	Hugh Biggar	Son	Unm	29	Foreman Joiner	Do
	John Biggar	Son	Unm	16	Clerk	Do
	Thomas Biggar	Son	Unm	14	Office Boy	Do
	Minnie Russell	Grand Daur		9	Scholar	Do
	Bessie Russell	Grand Daur		7	Do	Do
	Annie Russell	Grand Daur		5	Do	Do
	Margaret McLean	Visitor	Unm	58	Laundress	Stirlingshire Carronshore
	Robert Biggar	Son	Unm	18	Clerk	Lanarkshire Glasgow

Extract of an entry in the records for the CENSUS of SCOTLAND of   April 5th   1891

Held in the custody of the General Register Office for Scotland, New Register House, Edinburgh   1891/644⁹/26/22

Parish or district   Kelvin   City or county   Burgh Glasgow

Note: Particulars of relationship to head of family and condition as to marriage are not included in the Returns for 1841

Given under the Seal of the General Register Office, New Register House, Edinburgh on   20th July 1978

▲ A census return showing a lot of people living in one small house.

Having a family

Queen Victoria had nine children. Many other Victorian people had large families. Some mothers had a new baby every year.

In the 1860s, an average family had six children. Today, most families have just one or two children.

In Victorian times, many babies died. They often came from poor families who lived in crowded, dirty rooms which meant that illnesses and diseases spread quickly.

◄ Mr and Mrs Terry with some of their nineteen children.

Fathers

When a woman married, her husband owned everything she had. This was the law until 1882.

A wife and children had to obey the father. He was supposed to know best. Some men were very strict with their wives and children.

Most families were just as happy as happy families today. Mothers and fathers enjoyed bringing up their children.

▲ A Victorian father reading from the Bible.

Mothers

Poor mothers worked very hard. They had no help and no money of their own.

Middle-class mothers looked after their homes and their families. They often had servants to do the hard work.

▲ A father telling a story.

In most families, mothers looked after the children. Rich families were different. Rich people paid nannies to look after the young children. They lived upstairs in the nursery. Governesses taught the older children. The children went down to see their parents before bedtime.

◄ Children in a nursery in a big house.

Children

Victorian mothers wanted to bring up their children well. They read magazines telling them what to do. Some people said that children were naturally good. They should be treated kindly. Some people said children were naturally bad and had to be beaten to make them good.

In most families children were loved. But they were brought up strictly.

▲ In many families, boys were much more important than girls.

And see! oh, what a dreadful thing!
The fire has caught her apron-string;
Her apron burns, her arms, her hair —
She burns all over everywhere.

Then how the pussy-cats did mew —
What else, poor pussies, could they do?
They screamed for help, 'twas all in vain!
So then they said 'We'll scream again;
Make haste, make haste, me-ow, me-o,
She'll burn to death, we told her so.'

So she was burnt, with all her clothes,
And arms, and hands, and eyes, and nose;
Till she had nothing more to lose
Except her little scarlet shoes;
And nothing else but these was found
Among her ashes on the ground.

◄ Stories such as this were meant to frighten children to make them good.

Working children

Poor families needed money. So the children worked in factories, on farms, as chimney sweeps or road sweepers, down mines or as servants. Some children sold goods such as matches on the street. They often worked for long hours and the work was very hard.

Girls mending shoes in 1865. ▶

People found out how hard poor children worked. They were shocked. So laws were passed to stop young children working. After 1870, most children went to school. This helped the children but poor families missed the money.

Family gatherings

The family was very important to middle-class people.

Meals

The family met together for meals. Father sat at the top of the table. Mother sat at the other end. The children sat round the sides. The youngest child often said grace. This was to thank God for all the food on the table.

▲ Family tea in Victorian times.

Food

Middle-class families had good food. An everyday meal started with soup, then meat and vegetables, then pudding or cheese.

Family occasions

Families got together for christenings, weddings and funerals. These were often big gatherings. People could travel on the new railways to family gatherings.

Everyone wore black for funerals. A widow wore black for a year after her husband's death.

▲ A Victorian baby being christened in a church.

Christmas

Prince Albert, Queen Victoria's husband, set up a Christmas tree for his children. Christmas trees became very popular.

Christmas cards, Christmas cake and Christmas pudding are all traditions that began in Victorian times.

◄ This family is playing the dangerous game of snapdragon.

Entertainment

In Victorian times, there were no televisions, videos or computer games.

Victorian families read books, played games and sang. Girls learnt to sew. All the children made things such as pictures from shells and feathers.

Even quite poor homes had a piano. In the evening, the family gathered round the piano to sing.

▲ A family gathered around the piano.

▲ Table-top croquet. Croquet was a popular game in Victorian times.

Fresh air

The Victorians thought fresh air was good. The perambulator (pram) was invented in the 1850s. The whole family could go out for a walk and take the baby.

Poor children played in the street. Rich children played in their gardens. The older ones played tennis and croquet. In villages, men played cricket on the green.

Tennis was played by women and men. ▶

Family outings

In Victorian Britain, many people went to church. A lot of children went to Sunday school.

Sunday best

People wore their best clothes to church. Rich people sat near the front of the church. Poor people sat at the back.

Everyone sang hymns and listened to the sermon. Afterwards they talked to friends outside the church.

▲ Nearly half the people in Britain went to church every Sunday.

Outdoors

By 1840, cities had become very big. Most people worked for long hours. They only had Sunday free. They did not have time to go out of the city to the country. So public parks were made in cities. People could enjoy the parks without having to pay anything. Often a band played in the park. People also loved having picnics. Many people watched sports such as football in the parks.

▲ The Victorians loved picnics.

Pantomimes, circuses and music halls

Parents and children loved pantomimes. They crowded into the gaslit theatres to see pantomimes such as *Cinderella*.

Sometimes the circus came to town. There were lion tamers and acrobats.

Music hall shows became popular from the 1880s. There was a lot of singing and dancing, and people told jokes.

Films

The first films were shown in 1900. The pictures were jerky. There was no sound so someone played the piano during each film.

▲ Children dance in the street to an organ grinder's music.

◄ Punch and Judy shows were very popular.

Holidays

Bank holidays started in 1871. This meant that people had a Sunday and a Monday off work. Some people had never been very far from home. Now they could catch a train to the seaside or the country.

Middle-class families took longer holidays. They often went to Brighton or the Isle of Wight. They wore smart clothes on the beach. They wore nearly as many clothes when they went swimming.

Middle-class holiday-makers in the 1890s. ▼

Looking after the family

In Victorian times, men usually owned all the money in a family. The women ran the home.

More and more people wanted nice homes and bigger houses. They wanted good food and many clothes. So there was a lot of cooking and cleaning to do.

Middle-class women wanted to know how to manage servants. They wanted to know the best way to run a house.

Mrs Beeton

Mrs Beeton wrote a book about how to run a house. It was a best seller.

She wrote about everything from how to clean a marble fireplace to how to look after sick people in the family and how to make shirt collars shiny.

▲ Mrs Beeton wrote her book in 1861.

Victorian rooms had lots of furniture. There was plenty of cleaning to do. This Victorian doll's house shows what a Victorian house was like.

A Victorian doll's house. ▼

Servants

In Victorian times, there was no hot running water. There were no bathrooms, fridges, washing machines or vacuum cleaners. So big Victorian houses needed many servants. They had housekeepers, cooks, housemaids and kitchenmaids. Middle-class homes usually had one or two servants.

The maid's work

Many girls worked as servants called maids. A maid got up very early. She lit the kitchen fire, cleaned the hall and the family's shoes. Then she cooked breakfast. Later she made the beds, cooked the other meals and cleaned the rest of the house.

▲ The maid lighting the kitchen fire.

◄ A machine for polishing cutlery.

By late Victorian times, many houses had lavatories. ▼

Washday

In poorer homes, Monday was washday. All the girls helped. A metal tub was filled with hot water. The soap was grated into the tub. The clothes were rubbed and pounded with a wooden stick.

In richer homes, people had more clothes. This meant that washday might be once a month instead of once a week.

Health

Many young children died. Even in 1901, about one third of all children did not get enough to eat. Poor children were shorter and thinner than rich children. People born in the 1870s were expected to live for only 40 years.

A wash stand in a baby's nursery. ▼

Dirt and disease

Towns were very dirty. Rivers were filthy. This meant there was a lot of disease. In 1866, about 20,000 people died from cholera. New laws were passed. Clean water was piped to many houses. Sewage pipes took the dirty waste away from houses.

Medicine

Most people could not afford to pay for a doctor. They looked after themselves. Often they asked the chemist for advice.

There were all sorts of ready-made cures such as Whelpton's Purifying Pills. They were supposed to cure everything from sea sickness to skin diseases. Many people used home-made cures. For example, they drank mint tea to cure a sore throat.

How do we know?

We know about Victorian times because we have photographs and all sorts of objects that the Victorians used. We also have magazines, books and letters and diaries of the time.

◄ A Victorian medicine chest.

Glossary

Bank holiday A special day when banks and most shops and factories are closed.

Census A count of all the people in Britain.

Chimney sweep A person who cleaned inside chimneys using brushes.

Cholera A dangerous disease.

Christening A church service when babies are named.

Cutlery Knives, forks and spoons.

Factories Big buildings where things are made.

Governess A woman teacher who teaches children in their home.

Housekeeper A person paid to run a home for another family.

Middle class People such as doctors and solicitors.

Nanny A person paid to look after young children.

Nursery A room where babies and young children live and sleep.

Servants People who served or worked for richer people.

Sewage pipes Pipes to take human waste away from houses.

Snapdragon A dangerous Victorian game where people snatched dried fruit in brandy from flames.

Workhouse A large building where very poor people were sent to live and to do hard work.

Books to read

History Journeys: A Victorian Journey by Peter Hepplewhite (Hodder Wayland, 2004)

The History Detective Investigates: Victorian School by Richard Wood (Hodder Wayland, 2003)

The Victorians: Reconstructed by Liz Gogerly (Hodder Wayland, 2003)

Cruel Times: A Victorian Play by Kaye Umansky (Hodder Wayland, 2004)

Places to visit

Many museums and historic houses have displays relating to Victorian family life. The places listed below are a very small selection. Find out what is available near you.

Museum of childhood and The People's Story, 42 High Street, Edinburgh EH1 1TG. Tel: 0131 5294142.

Museum of London, London Wall, London EC2Y 5HN. Tel: 0207 600 3699.

North of England Open Air Museum, Beamish, County Durham DH9 0RG. Tel: 0191 370 4000

Museum of Welsh Life, St Fagans, Cardiff CF5 6XB. Tel: 029 20578500

Use this book for teaching literacy

This book can help you in the literacy hour in the following ways:

 Children can use the book's contents page, page numbers, headings, captions and index to locate a particular piece of information.

 They can use the glossary to reinforce their alphabetic knowledge and extend their vocabulary.

 They can compare this book with fictional stories about Victorian times to show how similar information can be presented in different ways.

 They can learn the stories behind everyday words such as *Christmas tree*, *pram*, *tennis* and *lavatory*.

Index